Inconsistency

Rachel Walt

BookLeaf
Publishing
India | USA | UK

Presentation by *BookLeaf Publishing*

Web: www.bookleafpub.com

E-mail: info@bookleafpub.com

ISBN: 9789363316133

First edition 2022

DEDICATION

To meu amor, ang pamilya ko, and the amazing
supportive friends I have.

A Tiny Flower

I found a tiny flower
crushed upon my floor.
I wondered how it got there,
so far from my front door.

The dry and flattened petals
were a rich dark purple hue.
My first guess was a raisin,
but that just wasn't true.

The tiny little flower
had a short dark green stem
that worked so well with purple
like a cozy little friend.

Thank you tiny flower
gracing my home tonight.
Your presence, though confusing,
is an absolute delight.

Just how did you get there,
so far from my front door?
Perhaps a gift from my lover
and his shoes upon my floor.

Rain in the Land of Sunshine

The static of rain
With the random heavy drip drip drop
Is quite familiar around the world

A howl of wind
And thunder a'rumbling afar
A cozy blanket for many

But in the land
Of desert beaches and eternal sunshine
Locals get confused

The slightest wind
Warm for parts that know winter
Cause the greatest chill

The light shower
From clouds light gray instead of black
Lack the heavy drip drip drop

The blessed locals
Gaze at the shower and decide
To stay inside

They say the roads
Are not engineered to be wet
Unlike other lands

They know not
That the engineering is a myth
And practice is truth

Demonita

A friend of mine I know from work
Asked of me a favor
She was to be sent to Japan
To be a Navigator

Her little child of fur did need
A place to stay a while
Her mother's place, her first idea
Proved to be quite the trial

For her mother had two cats yet
And my friend's cat could not
Find in herself to make new friends
How dare!? She'd rather rot!

And so to my place this cat went
To enjoy a solo stay
This little fluffy thing so sweet
Until it's time to play

For though she hated other cats
And neighbor dogs as well
She could not entertain herself
This little queen of hell

Try not to drag her feather toy
Across one's unshod feet
She will chase it with claws out sharp
Without missing a beat

And those claws they will get your foot
Without a thought or care
If you choose not to play her games
Then cat sitter beware

If you decide to keep her in
the house instead of out
Be ready for the constant meows
And claw marks on your couch

And if your window open stays
but think your screen secure
She will muster up her strength
Your screen's now on the floor

She will scale a wall in one leap
And explore the neighborhood
She will always spend hours out
Until it's time for food

She prefers to lay her head down
On the pillow where I sleep
I can't tell if it's for my smell
Or to remind me she's the queen

Now that she is leaving
Her presence will be missed
For a sassy cat is always loved
No matter how much you are pissed

Souvenirs for the Gifted and Accomplished

Something lingers at the edges
waiting for an opening.
It's usually quite small and easy to ignore
...Usually.

Sometimes.

Maybe.

Distractions help.

Sometimes.

Most of the time.

There are times when an opening
may remain vulnerable too long.
The thing at the edges
seeps towards the center.

Engulfing.

Drowning.

Searching for a Dream

Scrolling, scrolling, scrolling.
Double tapping.
Click the link and see what's new.

Remember what your strengths are.
Be reminded of what you're lacking.

Doom scroll until the screen
has burned a blurry image
across your weary eyes.

Do you want that for your life?
Or the freedom others portray?
Is that job a good fit for you?
Are you a good fit for it?

Siblings

Same background
Different personalities
Same love
Different goals

Both smart
Yet too optimistic for the world
And crushed
Everyday by unclear ambition

Different paths of similar service
Have led to similar physical harm
We attract the same broken people
Into our lives like the light to a moth

Gifted
But comfortable and without drive
My little brother
And I

American Dream is Pinned

Virtual pins are now the bricks
That build the American Dream
Each board a shrine to a wish of what could be
The aesthetic of perfectionists
Lusting for the unattainable
Rising costs
More pins over and over
Like and save and sort
Filtered dreams of shabby chic
You too can DIY
Then add a teal or rosy tint
Blur the lines so your crappy DIY
Looks like solid gold
To the hashtagged masses

Inconsistencies

Have you found them?
There is no set style or voice
In a poem

Just my rambling
Not even a consistency
In length

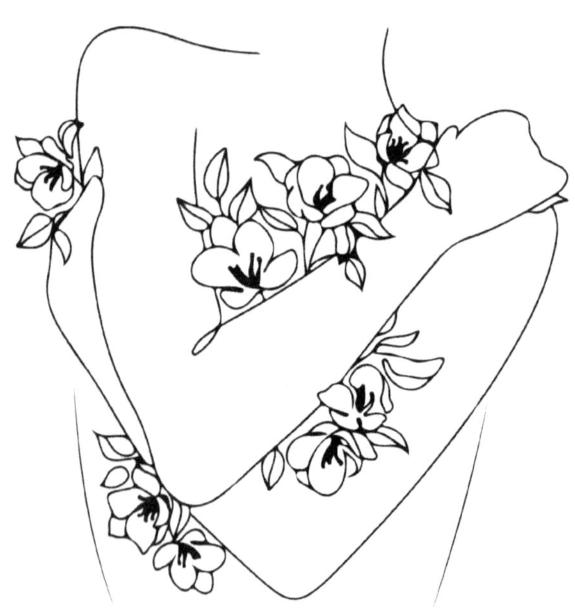

Slave to the System

If I want to buy a home
My sabbatical must end
A job offer must come
'Fore a broker can lend

Doesn't matter that
I've got a perfect score
A job must be at bat
Should I dare ask for more

I have earned this time
Budgeted and saved
Six months is quite the crime
"A job!"--the loan sharks crave

Meu Amor / Mahal Ko

Mahal ko,
Your love is so subtle.
Are you awake when
You drape your arm
Briefly over mine,
Checking on me?
Do you know I'm awake?
It's the sweetest little gesture.

Mahal ko,
Did you know
That I don't mind
When I have
My own sleepless nights?
It means that I can
Listen to your snores,
your dreams--
knowing you're asleep.
It's a comfort since you usually have trouble
sleeping.

Mahal ko,
I know you
Keep a list
Of the times

You've made me cry.
I keep a list
Of when you've me
The happiest
And most loved
I've ever felt.

Mahal ko,
Opposites can work.
I've seen it so.
I have faith
In our yin and yang,
Our fire and ice,
And all the
Other cliched images.
70 years with you,
My mahal,
Our long term investment.

Support System

No matter how many are in your court
It's not just about "having someone to talk to."
There are pros for a reason.
Darkness is nuanced.

In art, black paint is not used alone to depict
night.
It would come out flat.
Mix the black paint with another color,
And the depth of a real night sky is visible.

Shadows are not empty space
Waiting for a hero to fill.
There are things hidden
In what you see as a void.

An admission of struggle
Is not a cry for mass attention.
I love you all,
But understand I'm going to the pro.

Welcome Home

You are welcome here.
You have found your tribe.
You have found your help.
You have found a home,
Wherever you go.

I Am Not A Poet

I am not a poet.
My creative muscle is stiff.

What the heck

  Were

The

       Forms

I learned
          In school?

Please don't judge me
Former teachers of mine.

New Pants

Please for the love
Of powers up high
Just slip on up ove'
My ever thick thigh

Please fit well along
The curve of my seat
Please do not be wrong
Too small in defeat

The Weekend

Even when
Your days are free
B'loved weekend
A pleasantry

Should a plan
Arise for Monday
Regrets fill
The days of play

Family Diaspora

Modern problems
Of a family spread far
No longer at a distance
To travel by car

No longer so close
To just spend a few days
A vacation of weeks
And saving of pays

To afford such a trip
One needs a good job
That won't give the days off
Makes one want to sob

Wake

My heart gets a jumpstart
Waking up next to you
Your sleeping visage free
Of the stress you've accrued

Your breathing is steady
Like a calming song
Your face a rare art piece
That I get to look upon

And so I'll stay abed
For just a little while more
To enjoy the peace
Of each mini snore

The sun peeks through
dancing window blinds
You stir a little bit
Your first waking signs

Your long lashes flutter
And your brown eyes land on me
Your lips match mine in a smile
And I kiss your cheek

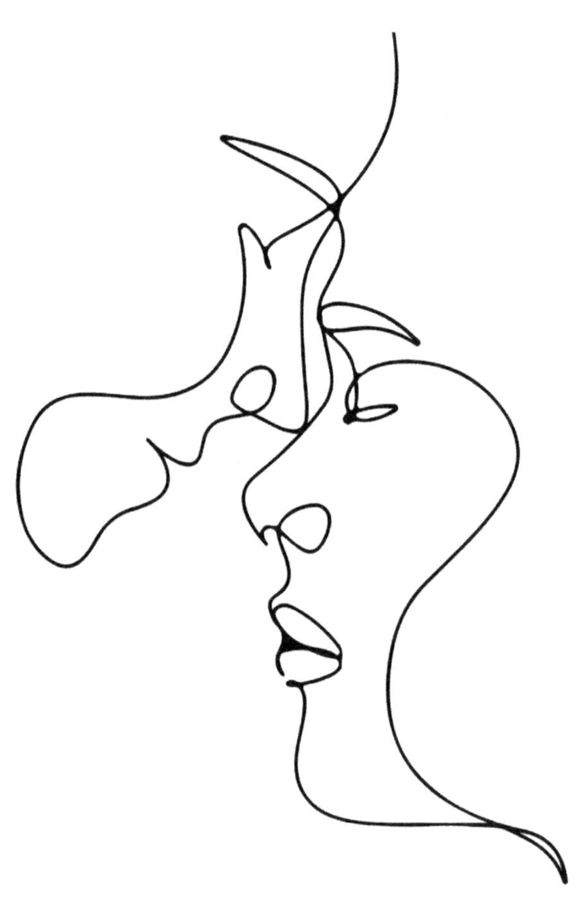

Unused Paint Brushes

Would love to return to
My creative days
When art class was fun
Or I'd doodle in a daze

I'm so sorry notebooks
And to the sketchpad
And watercolor pallets
Apologies, my bad

To the unused brushes
Do you feel too clean
Lost from your purpose
I swear you are seen

Golden Microphone

Poetry may not fit
And fiction books remain unwrit

Canvases keep their white
Sketch pads hidden out of sight

Pens scattered throughout the home
And washi tape tends to roam

But over ten thousand hours I endured
Stretching out my vocal chords

To sing in genres old and new
Local, international, solo, group

Many thought I would have sought
Fame and fortune and the lot

No I much rather prefer the lowkey
Hobby of singing karaoke

Family and friends gather round
A golden bluetooth mic's warped sound

Paradise

Heaven is a bed--
A dark room,
Window unit abuzz,
The air chilled,
Parents slightly snoring
On their respective sides,
Brother and I asleep,
Our eastern-style futon
On the floor at the foot of the bed.

Heaven is a bed--
Streaks of morning light,
Window unit silent,
But my bedside fan on,
Wafting air only to me,
Two of us slightly snoring
On our respective sides,
A cat asleep nearby,
Maybe one day a dog too.

Our Apartment is Hot

Our apartment is hot.
I admit it. You win.
Insulation is terrible.
It's rotten. A sin.
No benefit of sun.
It's dark. Should be cold.
We're the lowest unit.
Heat rises. I'm told.
So what the heck?